NKALKA

CW01304591

FORAGE &
MEDICINAL
WILD PLANTS

For rabbits and guinea pigs

Helen Knutton-Allcroft
NKALKA

NKALKA

I would like to dedicate this book to my family for supporting me through endless hours of research and walks to gather photographs.

Thank to those who have proofread the text
Ian Allcroft, Nichola Denton and Kate Walter

Publisher: Independent Publishing Network.

Publication date: 2020

ISBN: 978-1-83853-733-3

Author: Helen Knutton-Allcroft

Website: www.nkalka.co.uk

Please direct all enquiries to the author.

Printed by Enterprise Print

While every effort has been made to ensure the accuracy of the information given in this book, the author disclaims, as far as the law allows, any liability for any injury, loss or damage to either property or person or pet, whether direct or consequential or however arising.

I would like to kindly thank these people for their permission for photo's they have allowed to be used in this book.

Jack Raven Bushcraft – Hemlock and Giant Hogweed pictures & info, Nichola Denton – Wood avens, Gillian Eve Hawkins – Coltsfoot, Nadine Humphrey – Nipplewort, Annette Jones – Meadowsweet, Suzanne Kelsall – Cranesbill, Tara McManus – Borage, Penny Scrivener – Yarrow flower head, Pat Steele – Common Mallow flower, Shelley Stevenson – Wild fennel, Ann Thompson – Agrimony, all other photo's by NKALKA unless marked stock photo.

Front cover photo - Honley Woods taken by NKALKA

NKALKA

CONTENTS

NKALKA

Introduction

I have kept and bred rabbits for quite a few years now. My sister and I used to have them as children. I came back to rabbits when my children decided that they wanted pet rabbits, and, as quite often happens, the rabbits then became our rabbits and it evolved from there! My husband and I love their individuality, their personalities and watching them mature into beautiful members of our family.

Firstly, it is important to say, that I am not a professional botanist, mycologist or dendrologist - to be a forager you simply don't need to be one. When I started foraging it was to gather free and good food for my rabbits and guinea pigs.

Knowing and recognising the plants from my area is really fascinating and to know that I can give so many of them to our pets. Knowing they are safe and good for them is very rewarding to say the least. Hence, I would like to say that the plants in this book are ones that are found in the UK. I have not tried all of these foods for my rabbits and guinea pigs, although most have been tried. So, I would encourage you to do your own research and not just solely rely on one source of information. As with all new foods always start slowly.

Never give your rabbits and guinea pigs any plant you cannot positively identify.

I highly recommend that your rabbits are also vaccinated against

Myxomatosis, VHD1 & VHD2 as you are picking food from the wild.

Please note: The information about the plants and trees mentioned in this book is written with rabbits and guinea pigs in mind only. I have not referenced each and every piece of information, but I have put together a list of referenced pages at the back that may be of further use.

LEGAL FORAGING IN THE UK

You can find free rabbit and guinea pig food in lots of different places. Public footpaths, wasteland, woodlands, towpaths, riverbanks and bridleways.

You need to know which plants to pick – this is most people's problem. But before this you need to know the laws about foraging.

The laws governing the foraging activities are a bit complicated, because there is an individual right to forage bound to a set of intricate laws...

Foraging rules [2]

- do not deliberately uproot plants. All wild plants are protected by the Wildlife and Countryside Act 1981 and it is illegal to uproot any plant without permission from the landowner or occupier.
- only pick plants that you recognise and know your pet will eat
- pick plants from areas where there are large patches of the plant
- always pick in moderation so that plenty is left for others to enjoy
- be careful not to damage other vegetation when collecting forage
- if in doubt – leave it!

Theft Act 1968

The <u>Theft Act 1968</u>, for England and Wales, states that: *"A person who picks mushrooms growing wild on any land, or who picks flowers, fruit or foliage from a plant growing wild on any land, does not (although not in possession of the land) steal what he picks, unless he does it for reward or for sale or other commercial purpose."*

Byelaws on collecting [2]

The laws and regulations may vary between the four countries that make up the UK (The Isle of Man and the Channel Islands are not covered by UK law). Always check local byelaws affecting your area.

Some places where access is permitted will have byelaws which may remove or control some of these common rights to collect wild food. There should be notices displayed somewhere near the entrance. Local byelaws can be passed by councils, National Trust and government conservation agencies such as Natural England, Scottish Natural Heritage and the Countryside Council for Wales.

Good practices and good communication will keep you on the right path.
There are rules regarding foraging … please keep to them.
There is no substitute for common sense.
If you are not sure – DON'T pick it !

My advice to bunny and piggie parents that have access to weeds, herbs and plants in their gardens or out foraging is to choose 5-6 varieties that you recognise and know your rabbits and guinea pigs will enjoy. You can pick these in the knowledge that they are safe.

Never eat anything or give it to your fur-babies unless you are 100% sure it is safe and you can 100% identify it.

I highly recommend that your rabbits are also vaccinated against

Myxomatosis, VHD1 & VHD2 as you are picking food from the wild.

The information about the plants and trees mentioned in this book is written with rabbits and guinea pigs in mind only.

NKALKA

Code / key box

Picked for rabbits	yes
Picked for guinea pigs	Yes [1]
Pregnancy – red	no
When nursing	
May to October	✿

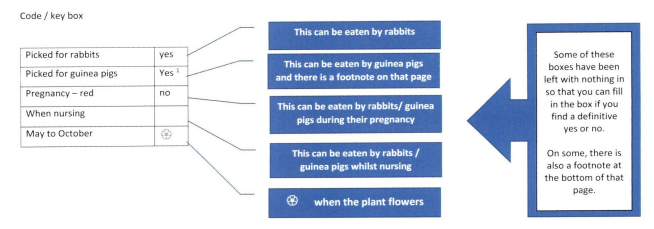

This can be eaten by rabbits

This can be eaten by guinea pigs and there is a footnote on that page

This can be eaten by rabbits/ guinea pigs during their pregnancy

This can be eaten by rabbits / guinea pigs whilst nursing

✿   when the plant flowers

Some of these boxes have been left with nothing in so that you can fill in the box if you find a definitive yes or no.

On some, there is also a footnote at the bottom of that page.

Please remember to make use of the GLOSSARY at the back of the book if needed.

Shortened abbreviations

URI – Upper respiratory infection   UTI – Urinary track inflammation / infection

A young rabbit's digestive system is sensitive. They require an increased amount of acid in their systems to handle feed efficiently when first weaned from their mother's milk. Any abrupt change in the type or brand of pelleted feed or the addition of a new foods such as fruits, vegetables or even grass in the yard can trigger an attack of diarrhoea which can be fatal in a very short period of time.[13]

Diarrhoea is the leading cause of death in young rabbits.

NKALKA

Agrimony *(Agrimonia eupatoria)*

Church-Steeples, Clot-Bur, Fairy's wand, Money-in-both-pockets, Salt-and-pepper and Sweethearts, Cocklebur, Guan Chang Fu Fang, Liverwort, Stickwort

Picked for rabbits	yes
Picked for guinea pigs	yes
Pregnancy	no
When nursing	no
June to September	☺

Info:

Agrimony is a perennial herb with small, star-shaped yellow flowers. The plant has a short rhizome with firm, hairy stems. The base leaves present in a rosette and the stem leaves alternate on the sides of the stem. The flowers and fruit grow at the top of the stem, burr-like seed heads, helping dispersal as they attach to passing animals. Agrimony is common in grasslands.

What it can be used for:

Partly due to its astringent qualities, it has many uses in herbal medicine including for ulcers, to stop bleeding and for gallstones. it can also be used for unsettled digestive system (Diarrhoea) and liver problems. It can be used as an anti-inflammatory and a diuretic. Also helps repel flies.

Additional info:

It has lots of vitamin B and K and contains Iron.

Birch - Silver *(Betula pendula)*

Info:

Several types of birch tree (Betula spp.) are found in UK. The leaves are non-toxic but not a favourite with rabbits. The branches and twigs may be offered for them to gnaw on.

What it can be used for:

Silver birch can be used to chew on. It is also used for pain relief, as an anti-inflammatory and as a diuretic.

Additional info:

Picked for rabbits	yes
Picked for guinea pigs	yes
Pregnancy	
When nursing	
April to May	✿

NKALKA

Birdsfoot Trefoil *(Lotus corniculatus)*

Info:

Birdsfoot trefoil is part of the pea family. A creeping perennial, with yellow flowers tinged with orange and red. It has long brown seed pods. It can be found in waysides and grassy places.

What it can be used for:

The condensed tannins of birdsfoot trefoil have anthelmintic properties and have been reported to decrease nematodes in wild and domestic ruminants (Min et al., 2003; Novobilsky et al., 2011; Waghorn, 2008; Molan et al., 2001). Birdsfoot trefoil was reported to decrease fly-strike in New-Zealand (Leathwick et al., 1995).

Additional info:

This plant is a good source of vitamins and minerals [29]. It is considered better and more digestible than alfafa.

Picked for rabbits	yes
Picked for guinea pigs	no
Pregnancy	
When nursing	
May to September	✿

Bittercress - Hairy *(Cardamine hirsute)*

Info:

The plant germinates in the Autumn and stays green throughout the winter months. The small white flowers are found at the top of wiry green stems.

What it can be used for:

It is a stimulating herb with diuretic and expectorant properties. It is best eaten though in January and February.

Additional info:

It is rich in Vitamins A and C and contains calcium, phosphorus and magnesium.

Picked for rabbits	yes
Picked for guinea pigs	yes
Pregnancy	
When nursing	
Mainly from March to August	⊛

NKALKA

Borage (*Borago officinalis*)

Info:

Borage can grow wild in woodlands and pastures. It is also a cultivated herb that many people grow in their gardens. with coarsely hairy stems and simple leaves, starry, bright blue flowers 2cm across over a long period in summer

What it can be used for:

Leaves have been traditionally used to make a tea to rid the body of a fever. The seeds are a rich source of gamma-linolenic acid. This oil helps to regulate the hormonal systems and lowers blood pressure, Borage also acts as a diuretic ana laxative.

Borage has a beneficial effect on the heart, adrenal glands, kidneys and the entire digestive system. It helps to sooth mucosa infections and can help reduce stress.

In nursing females, it stimulates milk production in lactating animals.

Additional info:

Just feed young leaves & flowers. Borage is rich in calcium, phosphorus and mineral salts. The flowers are very tasty.

Picked for rabbits	yes
Picked for guinea pigs	yes
Pregnancy	yes
When nursing	yes
June or July	❀

Bramble / Blackberry *(Rubus fruticosus & Rubus plicatus)*

Picked for rabbits	yes
Picked for guinea pigs	yes
Pregnant female	yes
When nursing	
June to September	✿

Info:

Brambles are often found in woodland and grassland. It has long, thorny and arching stems and can grow up to two metres or more high. Leaves are divided into three or five and dark green on top and pale beneath. Leaves and stalks are prickly. The flowers are white or pink flowers and appear from late spring to early summer, they are 2–3cm in size. The fruit, known as a blackberry, is 1–2cm in length and ripens from green through red, to deep purple and finally black when ripe from late July onwards.

What it can be used for:

It helps to stimulate appetite. It can help cool rabbits in the summer heat by increasing circulation therefore wonderful for pregnant does in summer / summer cooling.

Blackberries are high in phenolic compounds, which are known to be antiviral and antibacterial. It helps to calm down upset stomachs. Pick young & tender leaves and shoots.

Blackberries are high in antioxidants which are known to protect against inflammation, cancer, neurological diseases and aging.

Additional info:

It is safe to introduce greens for young kits use leaves and fruit.

It contains carbohydrates which includes fibre and sugars. Blackberry contains little fat, protein and water. In addition to vitamin C, blackberries also contain vitamin A, vitamin E, and vitamin K.

NKALKA

Burnet – Great (*Sanguisorba*)

Info:

In the UK there are 3 species of Burnet, all look identical with some minor changes in leaf size or flower head type. Sangquisorba minor Sangquisorba muricate, Sangquisorba officinalis [38]

Picked for rabbits	yes
Picked for guinea pigs	yes
Pregnancy	No
When nursing	No
July to September	✿

What it can be used for:

Great burnet is used mainly for its astringent action. It is taken both internally and externally and is a safe and effective treatment. The leaves are astringent, febrifuge, styptic and tonic. They are used in the treatment of fevers and bleeding. The root is a painkiller, astringent, diuretic, haemostatic, tonic and vulnerary. It is used externally in the treatment of burns, scalds, sores and skin diseases. The root is the most active. The root is harvested in the autumn as the leaves die down and dried for later use. Great burnet is an excellent internal treatment for all sorts including diarrhoea, dysentery and leucorrhoea. It is used in the treatment of peptic ulcers, haematuria, menorrhagia, bloody faeces and dysentery.

Additional info:

Stock photo

Chamomile – Wild / Pineappleweed (*Matricaria discoidea*)

Pineappleweed and Mayweed

Picked for rabbits	yes
Picked for guinea pigs	Yes [1]
Pregnancy	
When nursing	
May to October	✿

Info:

Chamomile grows in poor soil around foot paths, field entrances, waste ground and roadsides. If crushed gives off a not-so-pleasant odour, the flowers exude a pineapple smell when crushed. Plants can grow up to 18 inches tall and wide, though they are usually smaller. Chamomile has daisy like flower heads with 12 to 15 white, petal-like ray flowers, and yellow disc flowers [15] the foliage and stems emit a sweet smell when crushed. Pineapple flower heads are comprised of disc flowers only, with none of the petal-like ray flowers. [15]

What it can be used for:

Chamomile improves digesting food and is calming. It helps against bloated bellies, stomach problems, URI's and acts as an anti-inflammatory. It is a mild sedative, effective against anxiety and mild gastrointestinal upset.

Additional info:

It is a favourite with rabbits but seldom grows in large enough numbers to be picked regularly.

The herb carries very small amounts of minerals like iron, calcium, potassium, manganese, copper, and zinc.

---

[1] The whole plant can be used for rabbits but SPARINGLY TO GUINEA PIGS

NKALKA

Chickweed - Common (*Stellaria media*)

Info:

Chickweed is a hardy, small, low growing plant that grows in cool damp places. It is one of the earliest plants to appear in the spring sprouts in little white star like flowers. Found in woodlands and cultivated ground.

What it can be used for:

The whole plant can be used. It is diuretic and mildly laxative. It is often recommended for bronchitis, or congestion. Chickweed can also act as an anti-inflammatory, and help with healing of cuts due to it being an astringent.

Additional info:

It is a good source of vitamins and minerals with 6 times the amount of vitamin C, 12 times more calcium and 83 times more iron than spinach [39]. The plant contains saponins that, theoretically could cause problems if eaten in large amounts. i.e. can be safely fed in small amounts.

Picked for rabbits	yes
Picked for guinea pigs	yes [2]
Pregnancy	
When nursing	
early to mid-spring & autumn	✿

---

[2] Chickweed flowers maybe considered toxic for guinea pigs.

Clover - white (*Trifolium repens*)

Clover – red (*Trifolium pratense*)

Picked for rabbits	yes
Picked for guinea pigs	yes
Pregnancy - red	no
When nursing	
May to October	✿

Info:

The plant has an unsubstantiated reputation for causing bloat. It is a common plant in lawns and pasture grazed by wild and domestic rabbits without ill effects. This plant is a perennial.

Clover- red

Red Clover (Trifolium pratense) is larger than White Clover. Cultivated in meadows as well as occurring naturally in verges, pasture and rough grassland. It is palatable and safe for rabbits despite its (unproven) reputation for causing 'bloat'.

What it can be used for:

The whole plant can be used. It can be used as an antispasmodic. Clover also works as anti-coagulant.

Additional info:

Nutritionally, clovers have proteins, iron, calcium, vitamin C, manganese, sodium and vitamins A, C, K, among other nutrients.

NKALKA

Coltsfoot *(Tussilago farfara)*

Info:

Coltsfoot is a plant that may be seen on verges or hard bare ground. The yellow flowers appear before the leaves and resemble dandelions although the seed head is smaller. The leaves are large and angular and have the shape of a colt's (or foal's) footprint.

What it can be used for:

The plant leaves can help treat upper respiratory infection. It helps to sooth stomach and bowel problems and relieves diarrhoea.

Additional info:

It is rich in vitamin C.

Picked for rabbits	yes
Picked for guinea pigs	Yes
Pregnancy	
When nursing	
Feb, spring	✿

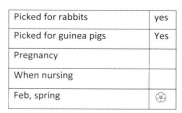

Comfrey *(Symphytum officinale)*

Picked for rabbits	yes
Picked for guinea pigs	yes
Pregnancy	yes
When nursing	yes
May to July	❀

Info:

Common comfrey is a hairy plant found on damp ground can be found beside rivers and ditches, on roadside verges, waste ground. It often grows in clumps. It has clusters of bell-shaped, pinky-purple flowers.

What it can be used for:

When slightly wilted is good for digestive aid. It is also good for healing and bone formation. The plant has a calming effect on rabbits. Also, good when a rabbit is off its food - it can help to get them back on it. Comfrey is good for pregnant and nursing does as it also supports the immune system. Comfrey is good for the stomach and can be fed as a general gut tonic.

Typically limit comfrey to ONE nice sized, young leaf, per rabbit/guinea pig, every other day or so. One large leaf is a significant portion of their diet. Comfrey should only be fed sparingly or when required. Comfrey is one of the best herbs for rabbits.

Additional info:

A useful plant, which aids healing but must not be fed to excess because of the alkaloids it contains. It is a great source of vitamin A. It can be cut down and dried like hay to store for winter use. In excessive feeding, comfrey can cause diarrhoea. This is its effects working too hard and if left unnoticed it may lead to dehydration.

NKALKA

Cow Parsley (*Anthriscus sylvestris*) - **NOT TO BE MISIDENTIFIED WITH HEMLOCK**

Info:

Cow parsley is a hollow-stemmed, tall plant that grows rapidly in the summer before dying back. It likes shady habitats and can be found on woodland edges, roadside verges and hedgerows with white flowers. These flower umbels (umbrella-like clusters). It starts to grow early in the spring and the new leaves are palatable for rabbits. It is always sensible to check the leaf stems for the groove that means it is safe to pick.

What it can be used for:

More than two fronds can make a rabbit hyperactive. Parsley root is a diuretic. Cow parsley root also helps aid in the removal of uric acid from the urinary tract and helps dissolve and expel gallstones and gravel — and helps put a stop to their future formation.

Additional info:

Unfortunately, hemlock is easily confused with cow parsley. Rabbits enjoy very much, so be careful to ensure you pick only cow parsley. Look at the stems. Hemlock has purply/pinkish spots on the stems, shinier leaves than cow parsley and is a brighter green – see next page for comparisons.

Picked for rabbits	yes
Picked for guinea pigs	yes
Pregnancy	
When nursing	
May to June	✿

Hemlock *(Onium maculatum)*

Info: the following info regarding Hemlock is taken from Jack Raven Bushcraft

Leaves - In this first Comparison photo 1 the cow parsley is on the left and hemlock on the right. The main differences are:
They are subtly different shades of green – the hemlock is a little darker.
Cow parsley has a matt finish whilst the hemlock has a slightly glossy sheen.
Hemlock has finer leaves, feathery in appearance.

Stems

In this next Comparison photo 2 cow parsley is again on the left and hemlock on the right. Whilst cow parsley often has a pinkish hue to the stem, hemlock has very distinctive purple blotches on a green stem. Make sure that you check the stem at ground level, this seems to be where the blotchiness often occurs.
Cow parsley is slightly hairy, hemlock has smooth stems.
Cow parsley stems have a groove, a bit like celery, hemlock does not have this.
In Comparison photo 3 & Comparison photo 4 you can see a cross section of the stems, again cow parsley on the left and hemlock on the right. Note, the photo is NOT of the main stems, but from stems coming off the main stem. Here the important thing to notice is the shape of the stems. Cow parsley is triangular whilst hemlock is round and hollow.

Smell

So, this is difficult to get across, but smell can help here as well. Cow parsley, I think, has a pleasant smell (a bit of a cross between parsley and aniseed), whilst hemlock really does not.
https://www.eatweeds.co.uk/is-it-hemlock-or-cow-parsley

Comparison photo 1

Comparison photo 2

Comparison photo 4

Comparison photo 3

NKALKA

Cow Parsnip / Hogweed *(Heracleum sphondylium)* **NOT TO BE MISIDENTIFIED WITH GIANT HOGWEED**

Picked for rabbits	yes
Picked for guinea pigs	yes
Pregnancy	
When nursing	
June and September	☺

Info:

Hogweed is a native plant (unlike its alien relative, giant hogweed) which is abundant in hedgerows, roadside verges, waste grounds and rough grasslands. As a member of the carrot family (an umbellifer), it has large, umbrella-like clusters of creamy-white flowers. Green to dark red/brown/purple, fleshy, thick, hollow stem and covered in small hairs. Its leaves are broad, hairy and divided. It is not as tall as giant hogweed.

What it can be used for:

Additional info:

Cow Parsnip contains sugars/calories in stem and roots and contain calcium and Magnesium.

Unfortunately, Giant Hogweed (see next page) is easily confused with cow parsnip/ common hogweed, which rabbits enjoy. Look at the stems, Giant Hogweed also has purple blotches on the stem and slightly shinier top leaf surface and dangerous.

Giant Hogweed, (*Heracleum mantegazzianum*)

Info: the following info regarding Giant Hogweed is taken from Jack Raven Bushcraft

!! Possible Confusion !!

Giant Hogweed. This is a dangerous plant with phototoxic sap which will burn your skin extremely badly if exposed to the Sun. It has slightly shinier leaves, more hair in a ring around the stem where the leaf joints are, and more flower stems, and is much larger when mature. Its hollow stem is ridged and purple-spotted, and its leaves are large and divided. Giant hogweed gets to 4 to 5 metres tall, common hogweed is normally around 2 metres or less.

Leaves

The leaves on giant hogweed tend to be divided, angular and pointed, whilst those of hogweed are more rounded. In Comparison photo 5, the giant hogweed is on the left-hand side, hogweed on the right

Comparison photo 5

Stem

The stem of the Giant Hogweed has distinctive purple blotches as seen in Comparison photo 7 and Comparison photo 6. There are no grooves and it is also hollow. The bristles are also sharp.

Whereas the Common Hogweed has only a purple hue to it as in Comparison photo 6. It also has a groove running down the stem and when broken it is solid inside. The hairs on it are downy and but not sharp.

Comparison photo 7   Comparison photo 6

NKALKA

Crab apple greens *(Malus)*

Info:

There are wild and garden varieties of Crab apple (Malus sylvestris). The wild varieties host a variety of wildlife and should not be damaged. All parts of the tree will be enjoyed by rabbits, but it is the fruit and the leaves that are most useful. The leaves can be harvested in the autumn when they are about to fall and fed fresh or dried for later in the winter.

Picked for rabbits	yes
Picked for guinea pigs	yes
Pregnancy	
When nursing	
April and May	✿

What it can be used for:

The fruit is astringent and laxative. The crushed fruit pulp can be used as a poultice to heal inflammations or small flesh wounds. The fruit is eaten to obviate constipation.

The bark, and especially the root bark, is anthelmintic, and soporific. An infusion is used in the treatment of fevers.

The leaves contain an antibacterial substance called "florin" [14]

Additional info:

It is also a good source of Vitamin C.

Cranesbill (*Geranium*) (*Geranium dissectum* & *Geranium maculatum*)

Picked for rabbits	yes
Picked for guinea pigs	yes
Pregnancy	
When nursing	
April to September	❄

Info:

Cranesbill can be seen in lowland hay meadows, roadside verges and grasslands. colouring the roadsides. It is also a popular garden plant that will grow well in sunny spots.

What it can be used for:

The whole plant, but especially the roots, is rich in tannin. It is antiseptic, highly astringent, styptic and tonic. An infusion of the whole plant, or the roots alone, can be used in the treatment of diarrhoea, gastro-enteritis, internal bleeding. It also works as a digestive stimulant and digestive aid.

Externally, it is used in the treatment of purulent wounds and inflammations of the mouth etc.

Additional info:

It is primarily the roots or the underground plant stems (rhizomes) of the plant that are used. Cranesbill root is best harvested as the plant comes into flower since they are then at their most active medicinally. Both are dried for later use.

The leaves should be harvested before the plant sets seed. The root should be harvested in the early spring while the aerial parts should be collected in the summer.

NKALKA

Dandelion *(Taraxacum officinale))*

Info:

Common Dandelions grow in all kinds of grasslands from lawns to roadside verges, pastures to traditional meadows, and can be a weed.

What it can be used for:

The leaves and flowers are ok to eat. Dandelions help the female to increase her lactation. Its diuretic properties can help urinary tract health and an astringent.

Root - improves digestion, reduces symptoms of bloating, gentle liver tonic, supports healthy immune system.

The flower heads help with pain relief and have anti-inflammatory properties.

It helps to improve appetite, it relieves gout and is anti-rheumatic, it improves liver problems.

Additional info:

Fibre is essential for any rabbit to have a normally functioning digestive system, they are full of fibre and high in calcium. vitamins A, C, and K. They also provide some potassium, iron, folate, and magnesium.

Picked for rabbits	yes
Picked for guinea pigs	yes
Pregnancy	yes
When nursing	yes
March to October	☼

Dock - Broadleaf *(Rumex obtusifolius)*

Picked for rabbits	Yes [3]
Picked for guinea pigs	Yes [3]
Pregnancy	
When nursing	
June to October	☺

Info:

This plant is considered as perennial weeds. It has alternate leaves with tough and unbranched stem. It is a weed in lawns, orchards, home gardens, roadsides as well as waste areas. The plant is generally found on borders of woods, floodplains, buildings, and poorly drained as well as nutrient rich soils.

What it can be used for:

On flowering, leaves contain oxalic acid which causes renal failure, young leaves only. It can have a laxative effect if fed in large quantities, it is an anti-toxin and liver/gall bladder cleanser. Also has skin anti-inflammatory properties.

Additional info:

Vitamin C, Iron, Vitamin A, Magnesium, Manganese, Copper

Dock leaves, are high in acidic content and phosphorus. They also contain a little calcium. Best fed to guinea pig before seed heads appear as oxalic acid levels rise in the plant after this time. If they happen to nibble one, then do keep an eye on them.

---

[3] Best fed before seed heads appear

NKALKA

Echinacea purpurea (Purple Coneflower*)*

Picked for rabbits	yes
Picked for guinea pig	Yes
Pregnancy	Yes [4]
When nursing	Yes
Throughout summer	✿

Info:

Echinacea is an herb that is native to areas east of the Rocky Mountains in the United States. A valuable addition to the garden although not generally found growing wild in the UK but still very much worth a mention here. It is an upright perennial with hairy, ovate or lance-shaped leaves and single flower-heads to 12cm across and brown central disk. Echinacea is perfect for growing in drifts among the border or among grasses.

What it can be used for:

Supporting a healthy immune system. Especially beneficial for animals who suffer from eye infections, upper respiratory inflammation (URI), and other health problems. It is an antibiotic, it stimulates the immune system and improves the lymph node system. Coarse texture of this plant helps promote proper tooth wear in rabbits and guinea pig. Guinea pig and small and medium rabbits – 1/2-1 tablespoon; larger rabbits – 1-2 tablespoons 3-5 times a week. Can be offered several times a day for a maximum benefit when treating acute conditions. Whole Echinacea Root is used to boost the immune system of rabbits and guinea pigs. Echinacea root can be offered every 3-4 hours for a few days when fighting has occurred.

Additional info:

Can be sprinkled on hay and rabbits and guinea pigs love whole echinacea plant. Can be used in addition to prescribed medications for a faster recovery.

---

[4] During pregnancy and nursing and the effects on guinea pigs [3].

Elder - ground (*Aegopodium podagraria*) also called Goutweed

Picked for rabbits	yes
Picked for guinea pig	no
Pregnancy	
When nursing	
June to August	☺

Info:

Ground Elder is a weed that annoys gardeners. Rabbits love it. It is a food source as it has a long growing season. It is a firm favourite to pick for rabbits, especially before it has flowered.
The plant is harvested when it is in flower in late spring to mid-summer and can be used fresh or be dried for later use.

What it can be used for:

Only the leaves and only until it flowers in June (not after). All parts of the plant are antirheumatic, diuretic, sedative and vulnerary. An infusion is used in the treatment of rheumatism, arthritis and disorders of the bladder and intestines[9]. Externally, it is used as a poultice on burns, stings, wounds, painful joints

Additional info:

It contains iron, copper, manganese, calcium, magnesium and potassium, flavonoids, which are antioxidants, saponins which have diuretic and expectorant properties.

Stock photo

NKALKA

Fennel - wild (*Foeniculum vulgare*)

Info:

Wild Fennel prefers drier conditions and grows everywhere from fields to roadsides but usually within a reasonable distance of the coast – although it is does grow a long way inland. During the spring, the green fronds sprout and grow throughout the spring and summer into tall cane-like stems that grow 60cm to 120cm. The flavour and smell of the plant is Anise or Liquorice, when you are cutting the plant the sweet liquorice flavours.

What it can be used for:

Fennel is excellent for bowel problems and helpful for digestive complaints. It also helps with bloating & gas. Fennel is good for milk flow of nursing does.

Additional info:

It is rich in vitamins and minerals.

Picked for rabbits	yes
Picked for guinea pig	yes
Pregnancy	
When nursing	yes
July	☼

Field Penny-cress (Honesty) *Thlaspi arvense*

Honesty, silver-dollar plant, money-plant

Info:

Short to medium hairless, erect plant. Stem leaves are oblong, clasping the stem closely, lower leaves stalked, not in a rosette. Flowers are white with yellow with 4 to 6 mm anthers yellow. Fruit quite large 10 to 15 mm rounded with a deep notch and broadly winged.

What it can be used for:

Both the seed and the young shoots are said to be good for the eyes.

Entire plant is antidote, anti-inflammatory, blood tonic, depurative, diaphoretic, expectorant, febrifuge and hepatic. Plant has a broad antibacterial activity, effective against the growth of Staphylococci and streptococci. Seeds of field Penny cress are used as a blood cleanser and as an agent in rheumatic diseases such as osteoarthritis and arthritis [40]

Additional info:

Young leaves can be eaten raw. They should be harvested before the plant comes into flower or they will be very bitter. The leaf is rich in protein.

Seeds are used in Tibetan medicine and are considered to have an acrid taste and a cooling potency.

Picked for rabbits	yes
Picked for guinea pigs	
Pregnancy	
When nursing	
May and June	

NKALKA

Garlic Mustard (*Alliaria petiolate*)

Jack in the Hedge

Info:

Picked for rabbits	yes
Picked for guinea pigs	yes
Pregnancy	
When nursing	
April to July	☺

Garlic mustard, also known as 'Jack-by-the-hedge', likes shady places, such as the edges of woods and hedgerows. It can grow to over a metre tall but are generally between 30 and 46 cm tall and has small white flowers. It is a biennial plant, so takes two years to complete its lifecycle.

What it can be used for:

The flowers, leaves, stem, roots and seeds can all be used.

Leaves and stems are, deobstruent, can be used to help destroy parasitic worms and healing of wounds. Leaves have been taken internally to treat / bring relief to congested chest, bronchitis and asthma. It can be used for stimulating appetite and inducing hunger. The leaves are also believed to strengthen the digestive system. Externally, they have been used as an antiseptic poultice on ulcers.

Roots are chopped up small and then heated in oil to make an ointment to rub on the chest to bring relief from bronchitis. It can be effective for keeping respiratory problems (anti-asthmatic) at bay.

Garlic mustard was once used medicinally as a diuretic.

Additional info:

It is a good source of vitamin A. Excellent source of vitamin C to help prevent scurvy (antiscorbutic).

Grass (*Graminoids*)

Info:

The grass is visible all year round. It is typically found across meadows and other grassy areas that are moderately fertile and moist. It can be found along roadsides and bordering hedgerows, but mainly in the garden.

What it can be used for:

The best thing for rabbits and guinea pigs both as food and tooth wear. It contains fibre.

Additional info:

Grass has crude protein and calcium in it.

Picked for rabbits	yes
Picked for guinea pigs	yes
Pregnancy	Yes
When nursing	yes
Late spring and early summer	❀

NKALKA

Groundsel (*Senecio vulgaris*)

Info:

The leaves are bright shiny green, long and raggedly lobed. The small yellow flower heads are in cluster at the ends of the stems appearing to emerge from little tubes. Groundsel is an annual weed of cultivated or disturbed ground, cropping up along field edges, roadside verges and on waste grounds.

Picked for rabbits	yes
Picked for guinea pigs	yes
Pregnancy	
When nursing	
Mainly April and October	✿

What it can be used for:

Rabbits enjoy the leaves and seeds - whole plant can be used unless covered in orange spots – appetite stimulator. It is helpful for healing internal injuries after surgery. A weak infusion of the plant is now sometimes given as a simple and easy laxative: it causes no irritation or pain [10]. Also, an antiscorbutic, diuretic and anthelmintic.

Additional info:

It was formerly used for poultices.

Contains oxalates (like spinach & strawberries) so not to be used if kidney stones are known of. It is high in Vitamins A and C. The plant is also high in Manganese, Calcium and is high in Magnesium, Phosphorus, Potassium, Zinc and Copper. Additionally, it contains fatty acids.

Hawkweed (*Hieracium*) - *Pilosella aurantiaca*

Picked for rabbits	yes
Picked for guinea pigs	yes
Pregnancy	
When nursing	
June to August	☺

Info:

Mouse-ear-hawkweed is a perennial, native in short grassland on well-drained soils. It occurs on calcareous pastures, heaths, banks, rocky places and walls, native in short grassland on well-drained soils; is absent from wetland. It does not occur in woodland or other shady places. Yellow or orange flowerheads.

What it can be used for:

Extract of mouse-ear-hawkweed has anti-bacterial properties and has been used as an antibiotic against brucellosis. It has also been used as an herbal treatment for respiratory infections. They may help control blood sugar levels too.

Additional info:

Rabbits rarely eat the rosettes but feed on the developing flower stalk and buds.

They are good sources of vitamin B-6, vitamin C, and potassium. High in fibre, and with a low glycaemic index.

NKALKA

Hawthorn / berry *(Crataegus laevigata)* Hawthorn *(crataegus monogyna)*

Picked for rabbits	yes
Picked for guinea pigs	yes
Pregnancy	
When nursing	
April to June	✾

Info:

Hawthorn flowers in the spring with a strongly scented white or pale pink flower. The berries (haws) are bright red but rabbits do not tend to eat them. Birds do, so the berries are better left on the bush for winter. No part of the plant is poisonous and can be picked at any time of the year. New spring growth is not thorny and is among everyday plants to forage in the early spring when forage is scarce. Later in the year they are easier plants to pick.

What it can be used for:

Stimulates appetite and aids digestion. Hawthorn berries are nature's safest heart and vascular tonics to help prevent heart disease in guinea pigs and rabbits. Hawthorn berries abolish some types of rhythm disturbances and are used in the treatment of congestive heart failure. Also, a diuretic and astringent.

Additional info:

A hawthorn berry is a good source of numerous nutrients, including vitamin C, vitamins B1, B2, B3, B6, B12, potassium, phosphorus, iron, zinc, and choline. Contain a significant number of bioflavonoids that enhance the absorption of vitamin C.

Hazel (*corylus avellane*)

Info:

Hazel is common shrub or tree that grows in hedgerows and woods. It prefers moist lowland soils. Although, it is not a favourite, rabbits will eat the leaves, young shoots and in the autumn, the bark of more mature branches.

What is can be used for:

Hazel – a popular feed, good for liver and biliary disorders. Chewing on fibrous plant-materials, such as branches, stimulates a natural grinding action of the teeth. This wears down the rabbit's teeth, keeping them at an ideal length, they also require to be chewed slowly which encourages proper salivation. This helps them digest their food better and aids in the release of nutrients from the fibre they consume.

Branches also provide fibre that helps keep a rabbit's digestive system in check. They're also incredibly nutritious for rabbits and help relieve gastric issues, GI stasis, constipation, and loose stools. Mostly, branches and leaves rich in tannin are excellent in preventing coccidiosis.

Additional info:

Chewing on rabbit-safe branches can keep your rabbit mentally and physically stimulated.

In humans, hazel's properties including its role as an astringent and anti-inflammatory compound, capable of reducing infections, speeding healing, protecting the hair and skin, balancing hormones, soothing pain and settling the stomach, among many others. [36]

Picked for rabbits	yes
Picked for guinea pigs	yes
Pregnancy	
When nursing	
mid-February	✿

NKALKA

Herb Robert (*Geranium robertianum*)

Info:

Herb Robert is common on waste ground and hedgerows. It can grow well in some parts of UK. Short to medium hairy plant often flushed with red and with a strong smell. Flowers bright pink 14 to 18 mm the flowers scarcely notched. Fruit usually hairy and ridged. A small modest plant up to 50cm tall. It has an aromatic smell when picked.

Picked for rabbits	yes
Picked for guinea pigs	yes
Pregnancy	
When nursing	
May to September	✿

What it can be used for:

The leaves, stems, and flowers are used to make medicine. Herb Robert is used for diarrhoea, to improve functioning of the liver and gallbladder, to reduce swelling (inflammation) of the kidney, bladder, and gallbladder, and to prevent the formation of stones in the kidney, bladder, or gallbladder. It is also used for diabetes, sinus problems, arthritis, high cholesterol, high blood pressure and cancer.

It is also applied to repel mosquitos and put on the skin for mosquito bites, parasites, arthritis. An extract of Herb Robert may slow the growth of bacteria and viruses.

Additional info:

It is enjoyed by rabbits and an easy plant to dry and store.

Some humans use Herb Robert as a mouthwash or gargle. The fresh leaves are chewed to relieve sore mouth and throat.

Picked for rabbits	yes

Knapweed - common (*Centaurea nigra*)

Picked for guinea pigs	yes
Pregnancy	
When nursing	
June to September	☼

Info:

Knapweed is a thistle-like plant (without thorns) that can be found on all kinds of grasslands from roadside verges to woodland rides, cliff tops to lawns. Has thistle type heads (but not prickly),

What it can be used for:

The whole plant can be used as an astringent and as tonic offer in small quantities.

Additional info:

NKALKA

Great Lady's bedstraw (*Galium album*) or Yellow Bedstraw (*Galium verum*)

Info:

Lady's bedstraw can hybridise with hedge cleavers, a white flowered plant, producing a plant that has features between the two parent plants but with pale yellow flowers.

What it can be used for:

Its main use is as a diuretic and as a treatment for skin complaints. The leaves, stems and flowering shoots are antispasmodic, astringent, foot care, lithontripic and vulnerary. The plant can be used as a remedy in gravel, stone or urinary disorders and is believed to be a remedy for epilepsy. A powder made from the fresh plant is used to soothe reddened skin and reduce inflammation whilst the plant is also used as a poultice on cuts, skin infections, slow-healing wounds etc.

Additional info:

Picked for rabbits	yes
Picked for guinea pigs	yes
Pregnancy	no [5]
When nursing	no [5]
May to September	✿

---

[5] There is not enough reliable information to know if Lady's Bedstraw is safe to use when pregnant or nursing.

42 | Page

Lettuce – Prickly (*Lactuca serriota*)

Info:

Prickly lettuce is an annual, rarely biennial weed probably native in waste places, rough ground, disturbed areas and on walls. It also occurs in cultivated fields and along roadsides. Leaves are slightly prickly on the edges. Enjoyed fresh – not as easy to dry unless you just pick the leaves. Flowerheads pale yellow. In Finland it is commonly referred to as "compass plant" because the leaves align themselves in a north-south direction while the surfaces run east-west.

What it can be used for:

The whole plant is rich in a milky sap that flows freely from any wounds. This hardens and dries when in contact with the air. The sap contains "**lactucarium**", which is used in medicine for its anodyne, antispasmodic, digestive, diuretic and sedative (**soporific**) properties as well as used in the treatment of ailments of the urinary tract.

Additional info:

It is also rich in vitamin A, vitamin C, vitamin E, and vitamin K as well as minerals including potassium, magnesium, iron, calcium and zinc.

Picked for rabbits	yes
Picked for guinea pigs	yes
Pregnancy	
When nursing	
July to September	☼

NKALKA

Mallow - Common (*Althaea officinalis*)

Info:

Common mallow can be found on roadside verges, along footpaths and on waste ground.).
Common mallow is a large, spreading plant with beautiful deep pinky purple flowers.

What it can be used for:

Certain parts of Common mallow are edible (leaves, flowers and seeds). Mallow is a
natural astringent, anti-inflammatory either for the urinary, digestive or respiratory
systems and emollient effect.

Additional info:

Vitmains A,B,C,E; mucilage; phenols; flavonoids; essential fatty acids; fibre; calcium;
magnesium; zinc; selenium; potassium.

Picked for rabbits	yes
Picked for guinea pigs	Yes [6]
Pregnancy	
When nursing	
June to October	☺

---

[6] Mallow flowers maybe considered toxic for guinea pigs.

Meadowsweet (*Filipendula ulmaria*)

Info:

Meadowsweet is a member of the rose family. This is a common plant that grows in damp places e.g. damp meadows and riverbanks and ditches. It has white highly scented flowers. Its leaves are sometimes covered with a bright orange rust fungus.

What it can be used for:

It was used to make aspirin (acetylsalicylic acid) for a painkiller. It can also be used as a weepy eye wash.

Additional info:

It is suitable for feeding to rabbits.

Meadowsweet contains tannins, vitamin C, sugar. The roots contain salicylic acid.

Picked for rabbits	yes
Picked for guinea pigs	
Pregnancy	
When nursing	
June to September	☺

NKALKA

Mint (Mentha), Peppermint (*Mentha piperita*).

Info:

Wild mint is an herb usually grows 10-60 cm (3.9-23.6 in). It has a creeping root. The leaves are in opposite pairs. The flowers are pale purple - occasionally white or pink. Mint thrives in rich, evenly moist soil and partial sun, where it grows to between 6 and 16 inches in height.

What it can be used for:

Helps to sooth cramps in the belly. Mint can help to relieve stress and anxiety. Mint helps to firm lose stools; it is a good herb for treating mastitis. It can be used for bunnies with eye inflammation. The liver can be stimulated with mint. It can also be used to relax the muscles of the digestive tract and stimulate bile flow, so mint is useful for indigestion, gas and colic.

Additional info:

Should be harvested just before flowering. Avoid prolonged use, it can irritate the mucous membranes.

Picked for rabbits	yes
Picked for guinea pigs	yes
Pregnancy	
When nursing	No [7]
Mid to late summer	✖

---

[7] DO NOT FEED to lactating does unless helping to dry up milk supply during weaning.

Nettle - stinging (*urtica dioica*)

Info:

Picked for rabbits	yes
Picked for guinea pigs	yes [8]
Pregnancy	yes
When nursing	
May to September	

Nettles are common in verges, meadows and grassy places. It is a good foraging plant as it is eaten readily by rabbits and dries easily.

It is best to dry the stingy nettles, but the ones that do not sting can be fed, all types of them (yellow, white or purple flowers).

What it can be used for:

Nettles are used as a diuretic, an anti-inflammatory and has natural antihistamines to relieve allergies. Nettles with white flowers work as anti-depressant. It is used to stop bleeding (astringent). Nettles are also a good source of antioxidant.

Additional info:

Nettle hay is a particularly valuable rabbit & guinea pig food, especially for those convalescing. It must however be carefully dried and free from mould. High in protein and iron. Also contains silica; potassium; vitamins A & C.

---

[8] Nettles should not be fed to guinea pigs with kidney and bladder stone problems, as nettles increase the intake of calcium.

NKALKA

Nettle – purple / red dead (*Lamium purpureum*)

Info:

Red deadnettle is a common wild plant that can be picked for rabbits. There are also many garden varieties. It flowers early.

Guinea pigs and rabbits love nettle leaf and stem.

What it can be used for:

Nettles are particularly good to help with lactation. Especially beneficial for animals who recover from illness and need extra vitamins and trace elements. Nutrients from nettle are fully available for uptake and utilization and do not put strain on liver and kidneys. Nettles also helps relieve diarrhoea .

Additional info:

It supplies guinea pigs and rabbits with important nutrients. Nettle is a good source of iron and vitamins A, C, D, K, B complex. Iron, Phosphorus, Magnesium, Potassium, Beta-carotene.

Picked for rabbits	yes
Picked for guinea pigs	yes
Pregnancy	yes
When nursing	yes
March to April	❀

Nipplewort (*Lapsana communis*)

Info:

Nipplewort can be found in open woods, hedgerows (it is frequent in cultivated fields and field margins), waste places and rough ground. The leaves are quite distinguished - spear head shaped with two smaller leaves either sides below.

What it can be used for:

It acts physiologically without stressing or alternating the normal function of bladder and kidneys. It is a cold and balancing plant meaning that it is useful in case of external or internal inflammation and when a tonic is needed. The plant is also traditionally known for its emollient and anti-inflammatory action which explains its use in mastitis (breast infection during lactation) and external wounds.

Additional info:

Traditionally Nipplewort was juiced (before flowering) and consumed fresh to stimulate the urinary tract in case of urinary infection or kidney infection.

Picked for rabbits	yes
Picked for guinea pigs	yes
Pregnancy	yes
When nursing	yes
June to September	☼

NKALKA

Plantain - Ribwort (*plantago lanceolata*), Common Plantain (*plantago major*)

Info:

It is distinctive in shape and can grow on all but the most acid grasslands all over the UK. Ribwort plantain is a common roadside and hedgerow plant. Plantain is a low-growing plant that often has broad, medium green leaves sprouting right out of the soil in flat rosettes. If left to flower, tall, thin spikes grow and tiny flowers appear that are almost indistinguishable. These flowers transform into the light seeds that are spread by the wind.

Picked for rabbits	yes
Picked for guinea pigs	yes
Pregnancy	
When nursing	
Spring until late autumn	❁

What it can be used for:

Plantain possesses anti-inflammatory properties: it is useful for treating and helps stomach problems, inflammatory bowel disease and upper respiratory inflammation.

1 leaf and stem; larger rabbits - 2 leaves and a stem. Can be given daily. It is also a gut soother. Pick the leaves only. It decreases tingly feelings, it is a natural antibiotic , it can be used extra for a cough or a cold. It has antiviral, diuretic, properties. The plant relieves itching and swelling from insect bites and allergies and helps to heal wounds. It is also an antimicrobial, antihemorrhagic properties.

Additional info:

Sprinkle plantain on hay for foraging fun. It helps to promote proper tooth wear. It does lower blood sugars, so it should not be given to guinea pigs that are diabetic. It is a good source of vitamin K, A Vitamin A/Beta Carotene, C, magnesium, phosphorus, potassium, folate, fibre and calcium. It contains high levels of Acubin which is a powerful anti-toxin.

Raspberry (*Rubus idaeus*)

Info:

Wild raspberries can sometimes be found along hedgerows or on waste ground. The stems and leaves can be picked for rabbits. Raspberry leaves are a favourite.

What it can be used for:

Pick young & tender leaves and shoots. Good for curing rashes, belly aches, helping to cure URI's and is diuretic.

The leaves can be used for bringing labour on if the mum is a few days over or babies are not arriving. It can ease labour that is in progress.

Additional info:

Raspberries are rich in many essential vitamins and minerals. For vitamins, raspberries have vitamin C, most of the B-vitamins (especially folate), vitamin A, vitamin E, and vitamin K. The minerals in raspberries include calcium, iron, magnesium, phosphorus, potassium, zinc, copper, manganese and selenium.

Picked for rabbits	yes
Picked for guinea pigs	yes
Pregnancy	yes
When nursing	yes
Late spring to early summer	☺

NKALKA

Rose – Dog (*Rosa canina*)

Info:

Is a variable climbing, wild rose species native to Europe, northwest Africa, and western Asia.

It is a deciduous shrub normally ranging in height from 1–5 metres (3.3–16.4 ft), though sometimes it can scramble higher into the crowns of taller trees. Its stems are covered with small, sharp, hooked prickles, which aid it in climbing, with 5–7 leaflets. The flowers are usually pale pink, but can vary between a deep pink and white.

What it can be used for:

Only the ripe fruits – they are good to strengthen an exhausted guinea pig after illness or pregnancy. They will help with healing wounds and fractured bones, they improve digestion, they are calming, they relieve stomach and diarrhoea problems and they are a digestive stimulant.
They also help with inflammatory disorders, arthritis and diabetes.

Additional info:

In history, residue products from rose hips have been used as animal fodder.

Picked for rabbits	yes
Picked for guinea pigs	yes
Pregnancy	yes
When nursing	yes
May and June	✿

Rosehips (*Rosa canina*)

Info:

The rose hip or rosehip, also called rose haw and rose hep, is the accessory fruit of the rose plant. It is typically red to orange but ranges from dark purple to black in some species. Rose hips begin to form after successful pollination of flowers in spring or early summer and ripen in late summer through autumn.

What it can be used for:

Rose hips are very safe and can offered daily to maintain good health and prevent the occurrence of diseases in rabbits and guinea pigs. Guinea pigs, small and medium rabbits - 1/4 teaspoon; larger rabbits - 1/3 teaspoon; rosehips can be given daily. Rosehip help the female to increase her lactation.

Additional info:

Rose hips are not only rich in vitamin C, they also contain a good number of bioflavonoids, citric acid, malic acid, zinc, Vitamins A, B3, D, and E.

Picked for rabbits	yes
Picked for guinea pigs	yes
Pregnancy	yes
When nursing	yes
n/a	☺

NKALKA

Shepherd's Purse (*Capsella bursa-pastoris*)

Info:

Shepherd's purse because of its triangular flat fruits, which are purse-like, is a small annual and ruderal flowering plant in the mustard family.

What it can be used for:

It is used as an appetite stimulator and diuretic. It is also known to have anti-inflammatory properties and help with uterine disorders. It has astringent and hemostatic properties. It has a good calcium:phosphorous ratio so is a good forage for guinea pigs and particularly helpful if your guinea pig has diarrhoea. It could have an anti-cancer effect.

Additional info:

High in B1, B2 and Vitamin C. Also provides Vitamin A and K as well as other vitamins and minerals.

Picked for rabbits	yes
Picked for guinea pigs	yes
Pregnancy	no [9]
When nursing	
Early spring through early winter	❀

---

[9] This plant should NOT be used by pregnant guinea pigs as it contracts the uterus.

Sticky weed (Galium aparine)

Many common names including Cleavers, clivers, bedstraw, goosegrass, catchweed, sticky bob, stickybud, stickyback, sticky willy, sticky willow

Info:

Picked for rabbits	yes
Picked for guinea pigs	yes
Pregnancy	
When nursing	
May to August	❄

Sticky weeds are annuals that have creeping stems that branch and grow along the ground and over other plants, attaching themselves with small hooked hairs, which grow from the stems and leaves of the plant. The stems of each plant can reach up to three feet or longer, and appear angular or square shaped, the leaves can be narrowly linear, the leaves are arranged in groups of between six and eight. They have small star-shaped, white to greenish flowers that are clustered together in groups of two or three and emerge from early spring to summer.

What it can be used for:

Stickyweed is harvested in May and June as it comes into flower and can be used fresh or dried for later use. It is used both internally and externally in the treatment of a wide range of ailments, including as a poultice for wounds, ulcers problem. It strengthens the heart and arteries. Sticky weed is a valuable plant and a good cleansing remedy, it supports the lymphatic system to detoxify the body and can be used as a diuretic. Helps with UTI's and bladder, kidney stone, irritation and excitement of the nervous system. The plant can help with congestion of the head and lungs due to irritation of the brain or bronchi. It can also help with irritation and inflammation of the eyes and skin problems.

Additional info:

NKALKA

Thistle - Creeping (*cirsium arvense*) Musk Thistle

Picked for rabbits	yes
Picked for guinea pigs	
Pregnancy	
When nursing	
July to September	✣

Info:

Thistles can be found on rough grass land, pasture, arable land, waste ground and roadsides etc, a common weed of cultivated land. It can grow to 90cm (2 feet) tall, white cottony leaves deeply pinnately lobed, the lobes spine toothed, woolly on the raised veins beneath. Flower heads bright reddish purple, large 30 to 50 mm, half nodding, borne on non-spiny stalks.

What it can be used for?

The leaves have been used as a tonic to stimulate liver function. The flowers and leaves are antiphlogistic. The plant is a febrifuge to reduce fevers and purify the blood. The root is tonic, diuretic, astringent and hepatic.

A paste of the roots, combined with an equal quantity of the root paste of Amaranthus spinosus (known as spiny amaranth or spiny pigweed), is used in the treatment of indigestion.

Additional info:

Fibre, protein, phosphorus, magnesium, calcium, copper, zinc and other nutrients.

Root of first year plants - raw or cooked. ... Leaves - raw or cooked. A fairly bland flavour, but the prickles need to be removed before the leaves can be eaten.

In humans a decoction (extraction by boiling herbal or plant material) of the roots has been used to treat worms in children.

Thistle, Sow perennial - smooth (*sonchus arvensis*)

Picked for rabbits	yes
Picked for guinea pigs	yes
Pregnancy	Yes [10]
When nursing	Yes [10]
June to October	✿

Info:

There are many varieties of thistles and none are poisonous. The plant secretes a milky substance from cut stems or leaves. Sow thistle often grow on newly turned soil, on waste ground or in crevices along pavements or walls during August. The plants can be tall - up to 1.5m high and all have prickly looking leaves.

The plant has the appearance of the common thistle, it is not as prickly and can be picked easily. The flowers are yellow not purple. It is not a true thistle and incorrectly called Milk Thistle which is a different plant. Sow Thistle is related to lettuce family not the thistle family.

What it can be used for:

The whole plant can be used. The leaves have been used as a tonic to stimulate liver function, whereas the flowers have been used to reduce fevers and purify the blood.   The plant is used to help URI's, sore throat. It is a laxative and antibiotic.

Additional info:

Leaves high in Calcium, Vitamin C (30-60mg / 100g dry) and mineral salts. Vitamin A: thiamine, riboflavin, niacin.

---

[10] A safe food for rabbits and guinea pigs of all ages but particularly nursing does and sows. [31]

NKALKA

Vetch - common (*Vicia sativa*) also bush vetch, bird vetch and hairy vetch

Info:

Vetch can be found in waysides, lowland areas, waste spaces, roadsides hedges and grassy grounds. The pea-shaped flowers, 10-18mm long, usually appear single or in pairs, on stems containing 4-7 pairs of narrow leaflets. The upper petal is often a darker purple with paler coloured wings. The stem has a tendril at the tip, enabling it to climb. It can grow up to 70cm high.

What it can be used for:

The whole plant can be used. It is good for nursing does (Muñiz, et al., 2005) and has been used to medicinally treat eczema and skin irritations.

Additional info:

Like other legumes, it is high in protein. Good for rabbits during the winter.
A good source of vitamins and minerals.

Picked for rabbits	yes
Picked for guinea pigs	Yes
Pregnancy	yes
When nursing	yes
June to September	✿

Wood Avens, (*Geum urbanum*)

Wood Avens (*Geum urbanum*) Herb Bennet, Colewort, St Benedicts Herb

Info:

Wood Avens can grow almost anywhere shady such as woodlands and hedgerows but found in gardens too. It is a long-stemmed plant with little yellow flowers.

What it can be used for:

It has various medicinal uses such as a tonic and antiseptic. It helps to stop bleeding and is an anti-inflammatory. The plant is helpful with the stomach and intestine problems.

Additional info:

Picked for rabbits	yes
Picked for guinea pigs	yes
Pregnancy	
When nursing	
May to August	✿

NKALKA

Willow (*Salices*) Goat willow (*Salix caprea*) It is sometimes called Pussy willow

Info:

There are many species of willow (Salix spp.). It is often found along the banks of rivers and streams. Small branches or twigs can be collected for rabbits to eat the leaves from and strip the bark. All species of willow are palatable to rabbits and can be dried for winter

It is a commonly found in woodland and hedges.

What it can be used for:

Pick leaves and branches and use them in a pain relieving capacity, it's calming and helps to stop bleeding. The leaves and branches will lowers fever (febrifuge). It can help to treat intestinal inflammation, diarrhea and stomach discomfort.

Rabbits will chew the bark off first and then munch on the inside for weeks. Willow may be fed fresh or dried.

Additional info:

A good plant to offer rabbits for protein and fibre.

Picked for rabbits	yes
Picked for guinea pigs	yes
Pregnancy	
When nursing	
February to as late as June	☺

Willowherb - Rosebay (*Epilobium angustifolium*) and Willowherb - Great (*Epilobium hirsutum*) also Fireweed

Picked for rabbits	yes
Picked for guinea pigs	
Pregnancy	
When nursing	
June to September	✿

Info:

Willowherb is common on wasteland and in verges. Windborne seed and branching underground stems (rhizomes). Some rabbits will eat it. Great rosebay willowherb has slightly hairy leaves.

What it can be used for:

The plant has been used for centuries to ensure digestive health. It is light and easy to eat, so ideal for animals with dental issues who may struggle with Willow or Hawthorn. Great Willow-herb was traditionally used for kidney and bladder complaints.

Additional info:

Rosebay Willow-herb is rich in Vitamins A and C ... it has ninety times more vitamin A and four times more vitamin C than oranges. Harvest the leaves, shoots and root in Spring and the stem and flowers in summer.

Yarrow (*Achillea millefolium*)

Yarroway, Staunchweed and Poor man's pepper

Info:

It is found on grassland and wasteland from sea level to the hills (up to 1200m). .
Yarrow is a common aromatic perennial plant found commonly throughout the British
Isles. Yarrow's pretty, little flowers, usually white but can be pink, cluster together in
tight groups to resemble flat umbrellas. Different colours are grown as garden plants.
The leaves are like feathers and are aromatic if crushed. It is safe and palatable for
rabbits.

What it can be used for:

Yarrow is used in a host of remedies, from healing wounds to colds and fever,
stomach ulcers and rheumatism. The plant can be used for the urinary tract
health. Yarrow has diuretic properties and will increase the flow of urine[12].

It stimulates digestion and helps against bloated belly. The plant
is a natural antibiotic, anti-inflammatory, antispasmodic, it's
good for the cardio-vascular system.

Additional info:

Picked for rabbits	yes
Picked for guinea pigs	yes [11]
Pregnancy	
When nursing	
late spring or early summer	⊛

---

[11] Yarrow flowers maybe considered toxic for guinea pigs.

Glossary

- Anthelmintic - Anthelmintics or antihelminthics are a group of antiparasitic drugs that expel parasitic worms (helminths) and other internal parasites from the body by either stunning or killing them and without causing significant damage to the host.
- Antihemorrhagic - agent is a substance that promotes hemostasis (stops bleeding). It may also be known as a hemostatic
- Antimicrobial - is an agent that kills microorganisms or stops their growth
- Antipyretic – see febrifuge
- Antiscorbutic - (chiefly of a drug) having the effect of preventing or curing scurvy.
- Antispasmodic - used to relieve spasm of involuntary muscle.
- Antiphlogistic - reducing inflammation or fever; anti-inflammatory.
- Astringent - An astringent (sometimes called adstringent) is a chemical that shrinks or constricts body tissues.[7]
- Atherosclerosis is a disease in which plaque builds up inside arteries
- Deobstruent - A medicine which removes obstructions and opens the natural passages
- Diaphoretic - (chiefly of a drug) inducing perspiration.
- Diarrhoea - is different than the soft, moist, shiny grape like clusters of "night faeces" that sometimes find themselves stuck to your rabbits' bottom. Diarrhoea that has or shows signs of mucus is an indication of infection and should be treated by a professional.
- Diuretic - A diuretic is any substance that promotes diuresis, the increased production of urine.
- Emollient - having the quality of softening or soothing the skin.
- Expectorant - a medicine which promotes the secretion of sputum by the air passages, used to treat coughs.
- Febrifuge / refrigerant / body cooler - reduce the heat of the body. ... is the simplest and most concise definition which can give, of the terms used to indicate medicinal effects. (Miller-Keane Encyclopedia and Dictionary of Medicine, Nursing, and Allied Health, Seventh Edition. © 2003, 2003)
- Haemostatic - (Medicine) retarding or stopping the flow of blood within the blood vessels; retarding or stopping bleeding
- Leucorrhoea - is a thick, whitish or yellowish vaginal discharge. There are many causes of leukorrhea, the usual one being estrogen imbalance
- Poultice - a soft, moist mass of material, typically consisting of bran, flour, herbs, etc., applied to the body to relieve soreness and inflammation and kept in place with a cloth.

NKALKA

- Purgative - strongly laxative in effect.
- Soporific - a drug or other substance that induces drowsiness or sleep.
- Styptic - capable of causing bleeding to stop when it is applied to a wound.
- Vulnerary - used to promote the healing of wounds, as herbs or other remedies.

References

(1) https://britishlocalfood.com/foraging-british-law/
(2) https://www.harcourt-brown.co.uk/gallery/Plants%20and%20vegetables%20as%20rabbit%20food/wild-plants-and-trees?fbclid=IwAR0t-fvVAoJrulHzpgrj_U3_HSm2DPISeGf7XeOykWe4B6BKlZYMhIO3nTM
(3) https://www.researchgate.net/publication/307659794_Influence_of_Echinacea_extract_pre-_or_postnatal_supplementation_on_immune_and_oxidative_status_of_growing_rabbits
(4) http://fuzzieskingdom.com/index.html
(5) https://www.homeopathyschool.com/the-school/provings/goosegrass/
(6) https://www.wildfooduk.com/edible-wild-plants/wood-avens/
(7) https://en.wikipedia.org/wiki/Astringent#:~:text=An%20astringent%20(sometimes%20called%20adstringent,means%20%22to%20bind%20fast%22.
(8) http://forums.rabbitrehome.org.uk/index.php
(9) https://www.plantlife.org.uk
(10) https://www.botanical.com
(11) http://rabbittalk.com/
(12) https://www.harcourt-brown.co.uk/articles/free-food-for-rabbits/diet-sheets/diet-sheet-for-rabbits-with-urinary-tract-disease
(13) https://barbibrownsbunnies.com/diarrhea/
(14) http://naturalmedicinalherbs.net/herbs/m/malus-sylvestris=crab-apple.php
(15) https://oregonstate.edu/dept/nursery-weeds/feature_articles/mayweed_pineapple/mayweed_pineapple_weed_email.html
(16) https://practicalselfreliance.com/pineapple-weed/
(17) http://www.actionforrabbits.co.uk/Toxic%20&%20Safe%20Plants%20v2.pdf
(18) https://www.naturespot.org.uk/species/field-penny-cress
(19) https://rabbits-uk.fandom.com/wiki/Feeding/Plants/Burnet
(20) http://guineapigscavyclub.blogspot.com/2014/06/guinea-pig-feeding-guide-herbs-more.html

(21)https://www.ediblewildfood.com/borage.aspx#:~:text=Borage%20can%20grow%20wild%20in,people%20grow%20in%20their%20gardens.

(22)https://rabbits.life/wp-content/uploads/2014/01/dandelion.jpg

(23)http://www.onlineguineapigcare.com/can-guinea-pigs-eat-dock-leaves/

(24)https://www.feedipedia.org/node/280

(25)https://www.guineapiggles.co.uk/article/foraging-free-food

(26)https://www.villasanraffaello.com/wild-edibles-foraging-guide-hairy-bittercress/

(27)https://www.guinea-pig-advisor.com/feeding/food-list/

(28)http://forums.rabbitrehome.org.uk/archive/index.php/t-219915.html http://forums.rabbitrehome.org.uk/archive/index.php/t-219915.html

(29)https://books.google.co.uk/books?id=Xzb0abDGIzkC&pg=PA32&lpg=PA32&dq=Birdsfoot+Trefoil+and+rabbits&source=bl&ots=95c93XH7Ib&sig=ACfU
3U1SDUwT9vEqD2aIF49Ov3OACq16ew&hl=en&sa=X&ved=2ahUKEwjY6s2Nz5bqAhU0pHEKHTbpDuE4ChDoATACegQIBhAB#v=onepage&q=Birdsfoot
%20Trefoil%20and%20rabbits&f=false

(30)https://www.theguineapigforum.co.uk/threads/comfrey.13255/1

(31)https://galensgarden.co.uk/herbs-and-homoeopathy/herbs-for-herbivores/milk-thistle-silybum-marianum/?bot_test=1

(32)http://guineapigzonline.weebly.com/

(33)https://www.lawnweeds.co.uk/weed-identification/birds-foot-trefoil

(34)https://www.permaculture.co.uk/articles/thistles-high-nutrient-weed

(35)https://www.healthbenefitstimes.com/dock/

(36)https://www.healing4soul.com/impressive-benefits-of-witch-hazel-for-wounds-skin-health.html

(37)https://medical-dictionary.thefreedictionary.com/antipyretic read both definitions

(38)https://www.thehayexperts.co.uk/meadow-menu-guinea-pig.html

(39)https://www.specialtyproduce.com/produce/Chickweed_9823.php#:~:text=The%20Chickweed%20is%20very%20nutrient%20dense%20having%2
06,dermatitis%2C%20eczema%2C%20skin%20wounds%2C%20rashes%20and%20more.%20Applications

(40)https://www.healthbenefitstimes.com/field-penny-cress/

Bibliography

Miller-Keane Encyclopedia and Dictionary of Medicine, Nursing, and Allied Health, Seventh Edition. © 2003. (2003, July 24/07/2020). Retrieved from the free dictionary by Farlex: https://medical-dictionary.thefreedictionary.com/febrifuge

Muñiz, M. A., Pro, A., Becerril, C., Sosa, E., Ramos, N. A., Gallegos, J. Á., & Hernández, O. (2005). *Fatty acids omega-3 in milk of rabbits does fed common vetch and sardine oil.* Retrieved 6 14, 2020, from https://cabdirect.org/cabdirect/abstract/20053160664

NKALKA

Index